SUPERSTARS
OF THE
NEW ENGLAND
PATRIOTS

by M.K. Osborne

AMICUS | AMICUS INK

Amicus High Interest and Amicus Ink are imprints of Amicus
P.O. Box 1329, Mankato, MN 56002
www.amicuspublishing.us

Library of Congress Cataloging-in-Publication Data
Names: Osborne, M. K., author.
Title: Superstars of the New England Patriots / By M.K. Osborne.
Description: Mankato, MN : Amicus, [2019] | Series: Pro sports superstars NFL | Includes
index. | Audience: K to Grade 3.
Identifiers: LCCN 2017057276 (print) | LCCN 2018006991 (ebook) | ISBN 9781681514901
(pdf) | ISBN 9781681514086 (library binding) | ISBN 9781681523286 (pbk.)
Subjects: LCSH: New England Patriots (Football team)--Biography--Juvenile literature. |
New England Patriots (Football team)--History--Juvenile literature. | Football players--
United States--Biography--Juvenile literature.
Classification: LCC GV956.N36 (ebook) | LCC GV956.N36 O74 2019 (print) | DDC
796.332/640974461--dc23 LC record available at https://lccn.loc.gov/2017057276

Photo Credits: All photos from Associated Press except Getty Images/Focus on Sport
8–9, 14–15

Series Designer: Veronica Scott
Book Designer: Peggie Carley
Photo Researcher: Holly Young

Printed in China
HC 10 9 8 7 6 5 4 3 2 1
PB 10 9 8 7 6 5 4 3 2 1

TABLE OF CONTENTS

GET TO KNOW THE PATRIOTS

The New England Patriots started in a league called the **AFL**. They joined the **NFL** in 1970. The Patriots have been to 10 Super Bowls. They won five of them.

Who were some of the Patriots' greatest stars? Let's find out!

JOHN HANNAH

John Hannah was a great blocker. He was big. No one could get past him. He was a rookie in 1973. He went to nine **Pro Bowls**. Hannah helped the Patriots get to a Super Bowl.

MIKE HAYNES

Mike Haynes was great on **defense.** He was quick. He was good at **intercepting** passes. He played for the Patriots for seven seasons. Haynes was the NFL Defensive Rookie of the Year in 1976.

Haynes was added to the NFL Hall of Fame in 1997.

ANDRE TIPPETT

Andre Tippett was known for his **tackling**. He hit hard. He has the most **sacks** of any Patriots player in history. He went to five Pro Bowls in a row. He played on the team for 11 seasons.

TEDY BRUSCHI

Tedy Bruschi was a star on defense. He knew how to block well. He helped the Patriots win three Super Bowls. The last one was in 2005. He retired in 2009 after 13 seasons with the Patriots.

Brady has gone to 12 Pro Bowls. That is a Patriots record.

TOM BRADY

Tom Brady is one of the best **quarterbacks** ever. He has led the Patriots to eight Super Bowls. That is more than any other quarterback. Brady has won four Super Bowl **MVP** awards. He has played with the Patriots since 2000.

ROB GRONKOWSKI

Rob Gronkowski is fast. He knows where to go to catch the ball and score. He holds the Patriots record for the most touchdown passes caught over his career.

Gronkowski has been to four Pro Bowls.

JULIAN EDELMAN

Julian Edelman plays offense.

He joined the Patriots in 2009.

He is quick. He is good at

catching passes. He caught

the game-winning pass at the

Super Bowl in 2015.

STEPHEN GOSTKOWSKI

Stephen Gostkowski is one of the best kickers in the NFL. He has played for the Patriots since 2006. He is their lead scorer. In 2017, Gostkowski made a 58-yard field goal, which is a Patriots record.

Let's watch and see who will be the next star of the Patriots!

TEAM FAST FACTS

Founded: 1960

Home Stadium: Gillette Stadium
(Foxborough, Massachusetts)

Super Bowl Titles: 5
(2002, 2004, 2005, 2015, 2017)

Nicknames: The Pats

Hall of Fame Players: 7
including John Hannah, Mike Haynes,
and Andre Tippett

Other Names Boston Patriots
(1960-1970)

WORDS TO KNOW

AFL – the American Football League; a league that played in the 1960s

defense – group of players that tries to stop the other team from scoring

intercept – when the opponent catches a pass

MVP – Most Valuable Player; an honor given to the best player each season

NFL – National Football League; the league pro football players play in

Pro Bowl – the NFL's all-star game

quarterback – a player whose main jobs are to lead the offense and throw passes

sack – a tackle of the quarterback on a passing play

tackle – to knock players on the other team to the ground so they cannot score

LEARN MORE

Books

Burgess, Zach. *Meet the New England Patriots.* Chicago: Norwood House Press, 2017.

Fishman, Jon M. *Rob Gronkowski.* Minneapolis, Minn: Lerner Publications, 2018.

Websites

New England Patriots—Official Site
http://www.patriots.com
Watch video clips and view photos of the New England Patriots.

NFL.com
http://nfl.com
Check out pictures and your favorite football players' stats.

NFL Rush
http://www.nflrush.com
Play games and learn how to be a part of NFL PLAY 60.

Every effort has been made to ensure that these websites are appropriate for children. However, because of the nature of the Internet, it is impossible to guarantee that these sites will remain active indefinitely or that their contents will not be altered.

INDEX